DRAGONFLIES
LIVED WITH THE DINOSAURS!

BY MARK HARASYMIW

Gareth Stevens
PUBLISHING

Please visit our website, www.garethstevens.com. For a free color catalog of all our high-quality books, call toll free 1-800-542-2595 or fax 1-877-542-2596.

Cataloging-in-Publication Data

Names: Harasymiw, Mark.
Title: Dragonflies lived with the dinosaurs! / Mark Harasymiw.
Description: New York : Gareth Stevens Publishing, 2017. | Series: Living with the dinosaurs | Includes index.
Identifiers: ISBN 9781482456493 (pbk.) | ISBN 9781482456516 (library bound) | ISBN 9781482456509 (6 pack)
Subjects: LCSH: Dragonflies–Juvenile literature.
Classification: LCC QL520.H37 2017 | DDC 595.7'33–dc23

First Edition

Published in 2017 by
Gareth Stevens Publishing
111 East 14th Street, Suite 349
New York, NY 10003

Designer: Laura Bowen
Editor: Therese Shea

Photo credits: Cover, p. 1 (dragonfly) Hawk777/Shutterstock.com; cover, p. 1 (footprints) nemlaza/Shutterstock.com; cover, pp. 1–24 (background) Natalia Davidovich/Shutterstock.com; cover, pp. 1–24 (stone boxes) Daria Yakovleva/Shutterstock.com; p. 4 Marbury/Shutterstock.com; p. 5 MARK GARLICK/Science Photo Library/Getty Images; p. 6 Nicolas Primola/Shutterstock.com; p. 7 Dorling Kindersley/Getty Images; p. 8 Hcrepin/Wikimedia Commons; p. 9 GermanOle/Wikimedia Commons; p. 10 Michael Rosskothen/Shutterstock.com; p. 11 Steve Bower/Shutterstock.com; p. 12 Margaret M Stewart/Shutterstock.com; p. 13 (top) Vitalii Hulai/Shutterstock.com; p. 13 (bottom) Gary Meszaros/Science Source/Getty Images; p. 14 Education Images/Universal Images Group/Getty Images; p. 15 Rostislav Kralik/Shutterstock.com; p. 16 BOONCHUAY PROMJIAM/Shutterstock.com; p. 17 Therd Kallaya/Shutterstock.com; p. 18 Catmando/Shutterstock.com; p. 19 JOSE ANTONIO PEAS/Science Photo Library/Getty Images; p. 20 AuntSpray/Shutterstock.com; p. 21 Paul Sparks/Shutterstock.com.

Printed in China

CPSIA compliance information: Batch #CW17GS: For further information contact Gareth Stevens, New York, New York at 1-800-542-2595.

CONTENTS

Words in the glossary appear in **bold** type the first time they are used in the text.

AS BIG AS BIRDS!

Imagine an **insect** so big it can barely fly through a doorway. That was *Meganeura* (meh-guh-NYUHR-uh), an ancient insect **related** to the dragonfly. It lived about 359 to 299 million years ago, a time called the Carboniferous (kahr-buh-NIH-fuh-ruhs) period. *Meganeura's* **wingspan** was as big as a seagull's, about 30 inches (76 cm) wide!

Scientists have many interesting ideas about how **prehistoric** Earth became home to such large insects. Read on to find out more about *Meganeura* and ancient dragonflies.

MEGANEURA PROBABLY SNACKED ON OTHER INSECTS, BUT MAY HAVE EATEN SMALL LIZARDS AND OTHER CREATURES, TOO.

AIR SUPPLY

Scientists think there was more of the gas called oxygen in the air during the Carboniferous period. While air we breathe today holds about 21 percent oxygen, air back then probably had close to 35 percent oxygen. This would have greatly affected insects.

An insect doesn't have lungs. It takes in oxygen through holes in its body, but less oxygen than an animal with lungs. However, more oxygen in the air during the Carboniferous period meant insects breathed more in. This allowed them to grow larger!

Arthropleura

THE PREHISTORIC WORLD

The centipede-like *Arthropleura* (ahr-thruh-PLUR-uh) lived during the Carboniferous period. It was more than 8 feet (2.4 m) long!

THIS IS A MUSEUM'S IDEA OF WHAT A FOREST MIGHT HAVE LOOKED LIKE DURING THE CARBONIFEROUS PERIOD. *MEGANEURA* LIVED IN FORESTED AREAS WITH LOTS OF WATER.

RULERS OF THE AIR

During the Carboniferous period, there were no big flying predators to eat insects like *Meganeura*, such as birds of prey or flying **reptiles**. In fact, *Meganeura* was the largest predator in the skies. It ate other bugs, some quite large.

Scientists believe that *Meganeura* became extinct, or died out, when oxygen levels began falling over time. However, *Meganeura's* dragonfly relatives did survive. These were the dragonflies that lived with the dinosaurs—and outlived them!

THE PREHISTORIC WORLD

Meganeura fossils have been found in North America, Europe, Russia, and Australia.

THIS MODEL OF *MEGANEURA* STANDING ON A LOG SHOWS HOW BIG IT REALLY WAS.

NOT ALL ENORMOUS

Not all prehistoric dragonflies were huge like *Meganeura*. Some were the same size as today's dragonflies. The earliest fossils thought to be true dragonflies, most similar to the ones we see now, date back 250 million years ago. Scientists guess what they were like by studying fossils and today's dragonflies.

Dragonflies have a long, thin body and two pairs of transparent, or see-through, wings. Unlike the giant *Meganeura*, modern-day dragonflies' wingspans only reach about 6 inches (15 cm) across.

pterosaur

THE PREHISTORIC WORLD
Pterosaurs were flying reptiles that existed 250 million years ago. Some grew as large as fighter jets! They probably ate dragonflies.

TODAY, DRAGONFLIES CAN BE FOUND ON EVERY CONTINENT EXCEPT ANTARCTICA.

DRAGONFLY LARVAE

Dragonflies hatch, or come out, from eggs that were laid in or near freshwater ponds and streams. After they hatch, they're called larvae, nymphs, or naiads. Their shape can be different, depending on their **habitat**.

Dragonfly larvae's coloring is usually dull and matches plants, dirt, and rocks in their watery home. This helps them hide from predators, including fish, frogs, and other dragonfly larvae. Their coloring also helps them hide when they hunt food, such as worms, tadpoles, and small fish.

THE PREHISTORIC WORLD
Prehistoric dragonfly larvae could have been as big as a frog!

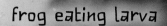
frog eating larva

DRAGONFLY ADULTS

As dragonfly larvae grow, they **molt** many times, becoming larger and more like adults with each molt. Their wings first appear halfway through their molts.

It may take a few weeks to 8 years for a dragonfly to reach adulthood. It depends on the species, or kind. After its last molt, it waits for its wings to straighten and its body to harden. When that's done, the dragonfly flies away, already on the hunt for food!

dragonfly molting

THIS DRAGONFLY, CALLED A DOWNY EMERALD, HAS JUST SHED ITS OLD SKIN AFTER MOLTING.

AWESOME ADAPTATION

Today's dragonflies have great agility in air, even on their first flight. This means they can move quickly and easily. Their favorite meals are small flying insects, such as flies. They catch them in midair!

Dragonflies' agility means they don't have many predators to worry about. There are only a few birds fast enough to catch them, including falcons and bee-eaters. Dragonfly speed was an **adaptation** that probably helped them survive being eaten into extinction by dinosaurs, flying reptiles, and other prehistoric creatures!

THIS BEE-EATER GRABBED A DRAGONFLY FOR A MEAL.

Fantastic Dragonfly Facts!

The quickest dragonflies fly as fast as 30 miles (48 km) per hour.

A dragonfly can move in any direction, and it can change direction suddenly.

Dragonflies have huge eyes. About 80 percent of their brain is used to see.

Dragonflies belong to a group of insects called Odonata, which comes from a Greek word meaning "tooth." They have big **jaws** and other mouthparts.

Dragonflies use their legs to trap insects to eat.

SURVIVORS

Dinosaurs died out about 65 million years ago. However, dragonflies survived. How? Some scientists believe dragonflies' ability to fly helped. Being able to fly allowed them to find other habitats to lay eggs if the water they hatched in dried up. And they could easily spread to new territory. Once they come out of the water, they sometimes fly thousands of miles!

Scientists also think a dragonfly's body has the perfect adaptations to hunt insects. No animal can **outcompete** them in the air.

Meganeura

THE PREHISTORIC WORLD

Scientists think *Meganeura* was too large to be a good flier. Was this another reason why this early dragonfly died out?

SOME SCIENTISTS THINK DINOSAURS DISAPPEARED BECAUSE OF AN ASTEROID CRASHING TO EARTH. OTHERS HAVE DIFFERENT IDEAS.

FLYING INTO THE FUTURE

Scientists can only guess what prehistoric insects such as dragonflies were like. Perhaps in the future, fossils will be found that tell us more about how these creatures survived so many millions of years.

In the meantime, some modern species of dragonflies are at risk of dying out. They face dangers because of polluted water in their habitats and water sources drying up or being built over. Will the animal that outlasted the dinosaurs adapt to survive again?

THERE ARE MORE THAN 5,000 DRAGONFLY SPECIES TODAY. THE HINE'S EMERALD DRAGONFLY IS THE ONLY DRAGONFLY ON THE US ENDANGERED SPECIES LIST.

GLOSSARY

adaptation: a change in an animal that better suits conditions

continent: one of Earth's seven great landmasses

endangered: in danger of dying out

fossil: the hardened marks or remains of plants and animals that formed over thousands or millions of years

habitat: the natural place where an animal or plant lives

insect: a small, often winged, animal with six legs and three body parts

jaw: one of the parts that make up the mouth

molt: to shed an outer covering that has become too small

outcompete: to win a challenge by working harder or being better than others

prehistoric: before recorded history

related: belonging to the same group or family because of shared features

reptile: an animal covered with scales or plates that breathes air, has a backbone, and lays eggs, such as a turtle, snake, lizard, or crocodile

wingspan: the length between the tips of a pair of wings that are stretched out

FOR MORE INFORMATION

BOOKS

Bradley, Timothy J. *Paleo Bugs: Survival of the Creepiest.* San Francisco, CA: Chronicle Books, 2008.

Owen, John. *#prehistoric: Follow the Dinosaurs.* New York, NY: Scholastic, Inc., 2015.

World Book. *Extinct!* Chicago, IL: World Book, a Scott Fetzer Company, 2015.

WEBSITES

Reign of the Giant Insects Ended with the Evolution of Birds
news.ucsc.edu/2012/06/giant-insects.html
Check out this site on insect growth in prehistoric times—and why they aren't large anymore.

10 Fascinating Facts About Dragonflies
insects.about.com/od/dragonfliesanddamselflies/a/10-Cool-Facts-About-Dragonflies.htm
Discover even more facts about dragonflies.

INDEX